Carpenter Gothic

Nineteenth-Century Ornamented Houses of New England

Text by Alma deC. McArdle
and Deirdre Bartlett McArdle
Photographs by Frederick L. Hamilton
Foreword by Charles Moore

Whitney Library of Design
an imprint of Watson-Guptill Publications/New York

First published 1978 in New York by Whitney Library of Design,
an imprint of Watson-Guptill Publications,
a division of Billboard Publications, Inc.,
1515 Broadway, New York, N.Y. 10036

Library of Congress Cataloging in Publication Data
McArdle, Alma deC., 1924-
    Carpenter Gothic.
    Bibliography: p.
    Includes index.
    1. Architecture Domestic—New England.
2. Gothic revival (Architecture)—New England.
3. Architecture, American—New England.
4. Decoration and ornament, Architectural—New
England.   5. Decoration and ornament, American—
New England.   6. Historic buildings—New England.
7. New England—Dwellings.   I. McArdle,
Deirdre Bartlett, 1954-   joint author.
II. Hamilton, Frederick L., 1900-
III. Title.
NA7210.M3 1978   728'.0974   78-8034
ISBN 0-8230-7121-9

Manufactured in U.S.A.

First Printing, 1978

Contents

*This book is dedicated to
Malcolm Pearson and Vincent Lisanti.
Their generous professional assistance
made it possible.*

Foreword

John Ruskin's nineteenth-century maxim "until common sense finds its way into architecture there can be little hope for it" is noted in these pages. With most of the twentieth century behind us now, we have had ample opportunity to note that until wit and verve and brio and tender memories (along with deep convictions) find their way into architecture, there can be but little hope for it, either. We live ourselves in an exciting time, when the past is coming again to be seen, not as a dead hand on our own creativity, but as an exhilarating source and stimulus, a connection that gives us strength and an enhanced freedom to make buildings that speak in many tongues, heresiarchs, and gigglers, to excite people of many moods and attitudes and concerns, to make concrete and stimulate our dreams.

It is the perfect moment to have come our way a volume of exquisite photos and descriptions of really liberated Carpenter Gothic buildings from the confident century which preceded our own. These unbridled enthusiastic gorgeous sincere heresies were made by carpenters who drew strength from the good wood and scroll saws in their hands and their own skill and were strengthened too by 700 years of heartfelt connection between the pointed shapes they were enjoying and God Himself. Everything was going, as this book points out, for these lucky carpenters. They were free of the strict rules which had limited their classical predecessors, liberated by a populist democracy, reinforced by a fervor formal and spiritual. Some of their support was in the books, and some of it was in the boards themselves, and the forests they came from. And from that double base of support they soared free—out of sight. I hope this gorgeous book gives not only pleasure to many eyes and minds, but the confidence that it would be all right 120 years later for us to try to soar, too.

Charles Moore, FAIA

Preface

I am a writer, not an architectural historian. When Frederick Hamilton and I decided to do a book on Carpenter Gothic, my version was simplistic in the extreme—his beautiful photographs and my amiable captions. The nucleus of the book was only twenty photographs, which Fred had taken as he traveled about New England on other assignments. He was convinced that many of these houses would be destroyed without a record, and he wanted to document them for himself.

Both of us busy with other things, a year passed. I continued to think about the book. Once, on location in Newport, Rhode Island, with another photographer Vincent Lisanti, I showed him some of Fred's pictures and asked his honest opinion about them and a book. Great! His reaction reassured me. Vincent knows what he is talking about.

Where to get started? An architect friend Lauren Meyers, Jr. suggested I read *The Architecture of Country Houses* and lent me his copy. I had never heard of Andrew Jackson Downing. It soon became evident that to do justice to the pictures there must be some kind of introduction to set them against their era. Mere captions would not do. My daughter Deirdre, now a graduate student in art history, was drawn into the project. Her solid, basic research provided the armature for the introduction which we wrote together. She also researched the section on tools. A frustrating job!

When the book was really underway, Fred and I took to the New England highways and backroads, he lecturing me on rock formations, I bickering about where we would stop for lunch, and both of us with an eye out for an inviting arch or finial.

It would have taken over a year to drive aimlessly around looking for some little gem. You do not find these houses clustered around the village green as you will saltboxes and central hall colonials. They are rare and sometimes a hundred miles apart. We were armed with specific and excellent information from the architectural surveys done by most of the New England states. The cooperation we received was unforgettable and is acknowledged elsewhere in this book. Sometimes we *did* luck out, as when we spun around the corner from the John Brown House in Portland, Maine, and spotted the William Goodwin House. And once again when a friend Leonore Merrick invited me to dinner at a famous harbor restaurant in Noank, Connecticut, and we passed the Peter Davis House en route.

As the manuscript took form (and Deirdre was back in Amherst with her own studies and unable to help except weekends) all kinds of questions assailed me. I found myself involved in architectural thought and terminology which even when I understood it, I could not verbalize readily. Terms such as "aedicular" do not trip lightly off my tongue. It was then that Susan Ryan came into my life. A doctoral candidate in art history at the University of Michigan and a research assistant at Yale, she took time from her dissertation on Yale architecture to assist me. Her extensive knowledge of the nineteenth century and her instantaneous grasp of what we were struggling to do brought the book into immediate focus. She introduced me to several important research books I had not read, pored over the captions, and made many editorial suggestions. I have not always followed them, so any errors are mine. Best of all, she has been enthusiastic and totally supportive of the project. Without her we would have had a book, but not this one.

Most interesting and revealing to Fred and me has been the delighted reaction of the people whose houses we have photographed. They welcomed our questions and, in many cases when they could not answer them, did additional research to help us out. In a region where the seventeenth and eighteenth century have always reigned, it was obvious that they felt perhaps their day had come. We think it has.

Alma deC. McArdle

Definition of Carpenter Gothic

To attempt a definition of Carpenter Gothic (also known as Carpenters Gothic) is to invite calamity. The term has been commonly used for years but never fully clarified. For the purposes of this book, it refers to any type of carved, wooden ornamentation used on American houses of varied architectural style, mainly before the Civil War.

Introduction

The Art of Building faithfully portrays the social history of the people to whose needs it ministers but cannot get beyond those boundaries.
                              Calvert Vaux, *Villas and Cottages,* 1857

The year Calvert Vaux, a leading architectural and landscape designer, and later a force with Frederick Olmsted in the creation of Central Park, made this modest statement, a visitor to California noted: "America is booming and statistics are broadcast to prove it is the most prosperous year in the history of the world."

Certainly a new exuberance had been abroad and broadcast for almost thirty years. It began in 1829 with the election of Andrew Jackson as President of the United States. "The wonderful beginning of the Age of the Common Man" is what seers of the time would say. Whether the President, himself, had any inkling of that when he fled the White House crowds on election night and took refuge in a neighborhood tavern, no one knows. But there was a tremendous wave of vitality and self-confidence in America. It was a time of exhilarating change. America was carving its peculiar geographical, social, and political identity.

The key to that identity was Jackson, the original populist folk hero. His election signaled a shift in American politics. In the words of historian Carl Fish, "Within the century public office and control of the nation's finances had been wrenched from the aristocracy."

Wishful thinking to the contrary, the old aristocracy still sat on the hill. But a new class—a bourgeoisie of considerable wealth—was being created by unprecedented industrial expansion. Most of this new middle class lived in or near cities; many had moved into a new space in the suburbs, far away from the farmlands which once supported the majority of the population. An exciting way of life was unfolding before them as new industries inundated them with reading material and cheap, mass-produced luxuries—from china and artistic reproductions to rugs. (By the 1830s for example, books were so much a part of family life, that the bookcase was a common item of furniture.) In 1844 the first wallpaper printing machine had been imported from England. A year later Elias Howe invented the sewing machine. And in 1848 Erastus Bigelow perfected a power loom to weave Brussels and tapestry carpets, thereby setting thousands of parlor floors abloom with larger-than-life roses and other exotica. Home decorating industries thrived, and 1850 saw the first magazine columns on the subject.

Between 1840 and 1860 the manufacturing value of factory-made furniture and upholstered items rose from 7.7 million to 28 million dollars. Thousands of chairs sold for as little as $1 each and "cottage furniture" (now classified "antique") was the Grand Rapids speciality of its day.

It was a complex and contradictory time, but when in the short history of America had so many fascinating options been open to the common citizen? Women's rights, abolition of slavery, temperance, and care for the indigent, insane, and aged were major concerns of the period.

In the 1830s public primary schools were organized throughout the eastern United States. Within the next decade an effort was made to standardize the procedures of these schools, and the first teacher-training programs were begun. Opportunities for self-improvement abounded and adult education courses flourished, ranging from the lectures of the Lyceum movement to the publication of such treatises as *Laws of Etiquette of a Gentleman*. The articles on manners, home decoration, and dressmaking, which appeared in *Godey's Lady's Book* and *The Home Journal*, to name two examples, regularized appearance and decorum. Social divisions were further erased by these innovations.

With unequaled opportunities came rampant avarice. Texas and California were annexed. The Indians were driven from their land and the foundations for great personal fortunes were laid. Fortunately, material advancement was partially matched by intellectual and spiritual progress. As David Carew Huntington pointed out in his exhibition catalog, *Art and the Excited Spirit* (1972): "Our ancestor who lived in the years between 1812 and 1860 perceived the universe as a vast moral theater. His eyes were ceaselessly on the watch for the glimmer or the glow of God's signature, his ears were ceaselessly on the alert for the whisper or the thunder of God's voice. At no time in our history has the human soul asked so much of its artists as it did in the half century between 1815 and 1865, the years of our romantic period. The country lived in a state of mind which depended to an unprecedented degree upon visual sustenance."

The painters and writers of the period reflected two dominant interests—a reverence for nature and concern for the lot of the common man. The poems of William Cullen Bryant and Henry Wadsworth Longfellow enjoyed huge popularity as did paintings by Asher Durand, George Catlin, William Sidney Mount, and Thomas Cole.

The theater, too, felt the impact of the need for visual stimulation and it drew wildly responsive audiences. When Charles Dickens toured this country giving his renowned readings from his own books, ladies wept, fainted, and some tried to tear off a piece of his clothing as a souvenir. At times his life was in jeopardy. In 1849 when a famous English actor William Macready appeared in New York, angry crowds rioted because American actor William Forrest had been poorly received in Great Britain. Known as the "Astor Place riot," this was one of the earliest occasions in America when police force was used to preserve order. During this period, the first opera house—the Metropolitan—was founded, and European artists began performing in the United States. In 1840 the Viennese ballerina Fanny Essler conquered New York, and the exquisite Jenny Lind (aided by the redoubtable Mr. P. T. Barnum) is said to have tucked $17,500 a week into her reticule while performing in America.

But even with the exchange of artists and the experiences of American painters and sculptors who apprenticed in European ateliers, the native landscape and typical genre scenes became increasingly strong influences upon the subject matter of both art and literature. Prophetically, the immense and varied landscape emerged as the one dominant and unifying theme in American art. This theme, which would shape and absorb members of subsequent generations as well, could not help but spill over into the architecture of the times.

So here was a young country with a predominantly young population eager for everything it could pluck from life and living. (After all the average life expectancy in the United States then was thirty-nine years.) And nineteenth century America in the throes of prodigious growth was ripe for the plucking. New ideas, inventions, and crazy fads spread across the country almost daily, and the nation's architecture was not immune. It, too, entered into a highly eclectic era. Architects and artists of the period did not despair, however. Even if the current architecture was derivative, drawing on every source from Italian to Egyptian, they felt it would eventually evolve into a style suitable to American life and regional climate.

For the average citizen—heretofore the invisible segment—there were irresistible affectations to deal with. Wrote Carl Fish: " . . . the use of carpets, ease of heating, cherishings of personality by daguerrotype and cheapening of kitchen supplies . . . decreased the difference between the homes of the rich and the poor (except in the case of the frontier)." In the future this middle class of wage earners would determine the course of American manufacturing and become the great social leveler of American society aided, of course, by the industrial revolution.

Andrew Jackson Downing (1815-1852).

Andrew Jackson Downing and the Influences of Gothic Revival

Although there were few architects, there were many books to guide the burgeoning homeowner, among them Asher Benjamin's *House Carpenter* (1839) and Edward Shaw's *Civil Architecture* (1834). Until the 1840s the popular fancy had been for the Greek Revival, and domestic architecture was marked by its imitation of the pillars and porticoes of ancient temples. Builders' guide books gave precise instructions for reproducing the classical orders, and these instructions were followed to the letter by carpenters.

In the 1840s, however, the Greek Revival style began to fade as it had already done in Great Britain. If the art of building reflected the social history of time, what kinds of houses were the new breed yearning for? Exuberant, of course, conforming, of course. For the public taste was too new to be independent. And while it might scorn the opinion of the aristocracy on the hill, the public was still too insecure to set its own style. It needed a leader, a prophet, in fact, and as often happens with prophets, such a man turned up in the right place at the right time. His name was Andrew Jackson Downing and he became the leading tastemaker of his day.

A self-trained landscape architect and a recognized horticulturist while he was still in his twenties, Downing's first book on house design, *Cottage Residences*, appeared in 1842

Design II from Andrew Jackson
Downing's *Cottage Residences*.

and was immediately successful. Much of the credit goes to his friend and close collaborator, the talented architect Alexander Jackson Davis who supplied many of the designs and renderings for Downing's books. But it was Mr. Downing, a magnetic young man with large, luminous eyes and long, dark hair who impressed the rightness of the style upon his readers and launched the Gothic Revival in the United States.

Cottage Residences was a book not only of designs but of architectural philosophy. Downing wanted to create what he considered the right rural or country style for middle-income families, an approach which produced the first suburban lifestyle. Downing's next and most successful book was *The Architecture of Country Houses* published in 1850, which went through nine printings and sold 16,000 copies. With this best-seller, he became known as America's principal proponent of the Gothic Revival in domestic architecture. His eloquent expression and romantic appearance turned him into a celebrity as well.

Between *Cottage Residences* and *The Architecture of Country Houses*, Downing had been exposed to and heavily influenced by the ideas of John Ruskin and Augustus Welby Northmore Pugin, the Gothic movement's principal English theorist. Pugin's ideas were familiar in the United States through his work, *Contrasts* (1836), as were Ruskin's, whose writing on aesthetics and architecture was hailed in this country.

The Gothic Revival in architecture began in England as an offshoot of the Picturesque movement, which was a revolt against the rigid demands of classic forms. This artistic rebellion, a century-long in foment and involving more writers and painters than architects, railed against formal gardens, symmetrical buildings, and imposing classic order on the natural landscape. The dissension also took other paths. One of these found its focus in philosophical discourse. It was here that Pugin's ideas were preeminent.

Pugin, a Roman Catholic convert, discovered in Gothic architecture the physical expression of his intense religious fervor. His justification of the Gothic was largely based upon the moral correctness of the style. Pugin argued that classicism was pagan. Gothic was moral (ergo Christian) since it did not impose rigid orders upon the design, but left the architect room to adapt design to purpose. Pugin's vision of Gothic as the perfect marriage of the functional and the beautiful was one of the foundations of Downing's ideology.

The effect of the Picturesque movement on American architecture is summed up by writer and historian James Early: "The architectural revolution engendered by Downing and other advocates of the picturesque brought a radical change to the shapes and plans of ordinary American houses; the first really profound change since the introduction of classical principles in the last quarter of the seventeenth century. For nearly 175 years, regularity, simplicity and symmetry had been the ideals of American builders. Now the picturesque taste made geometrical regularity of form an anathema. Houses burst out of the traditional rectangular molds in varied shapes and many directions. Irregularity grew in the interior arrangement of spaces as well as the creation of arrestingly jagged exterior silhouettes. The classical insistence upon symmetry of ordered elements steadily lost force."

If Downing was swayed by the power of Pugin's thought, he was also very influenced by the utilitarian ideas of John Claudius Loudon. Loudon's massive *Encyclopaedia of Cottage, Farm and Villa Architecture and Furniture* (1835) had 2,000 illustrations and covered every design topic any homeowner could possibly consider, from country inns to wallpaper to parochial schools. As Downing was to do, Loudon not only showed the overall plans of houses but discussed in minute detail how to build them, heat them, furnish them, and plant the surrounding grounds. As a very young man Downing had been exposed to Loudon's ideas through an English friend. It is possible he felt an immediate rapport with him, since like Loudon, Downing's primary concern was with the middle-class family.

Downing's views were strong and he was not timid about expressing them. In the preface to *The Architecture of Country Houses* he wrote: "There are three excellent reasons why my countrymen should have good houses. The first is because a good house (and by this I mean a fitting, tasteful and significant dwelling) is a powerful means of civilization. A nation whose rural population is content to live in mean huts and miserable hovels is certain to be behind its neighbors in education, the arts and all that make up the external signs of progress. With the perception of proportion, symmetry, order and beauty awakens the desire for possession and with them comes that refinement of manners which distinguishes a civilized from a coarse and brutal people. So long as men are forced to dwell in log huts and follow a hunter's life, we must not be surprised at lynch law and the use of the bowie knife. But when smiling lawns and tasteful cottages begin to embellish a country, we know that order and culture are established."

The designs in Downing's books could only loosely be termed "Gothic." Downing and the architects such as Gervase Wheeler and John Notman, who contributed to his books, freely interpreted the style, drawing primarily upon its picturesque qualities. They explored, in the words of art historian Vincent Scully, " . . . the possibilities of an architecture based upon the dynamics of interwoven members rather than the stasis of cubical masses."

Function, Suitability, and Honesty in Design

Many designs utilized board-and-batten construction, a batten being a thin strip of wood used to cover the joining of vertical boards. It was a type of construction especially pleasing to Downing et al. because in the Puginian sense it was honest and true, not attempting to imitate any other material, such as freestone or brick. A.J. Davis, one of the first to propose this type of construction in the Western world, and Downing, who enthusiastically endorsed the idea, could scarcely have foreseen its impact on architects of the future. Scully credits board-and-batten construction with providing a new vertical emphasis in design. Other critics go further, claiming that it prevailed until the moment of Frank Lloyd Wright and even beyond to the country's first skyscrapers.

The majority of the houses portrayed in Downing's books were by his definition either the "rural Gothic," distinguished by pointed roof and window gables, or "Italianate," possessing projecting roofs, balconies, and terraces. Most of the designs also included wide porches and/or balconies, for Downing

18

House, Clinton, Connecticut.

hoped to provide a harmonious relationship between house and landscape. In this connection he felt houses should always be painted in the subdued tones of leaf, stone, and bark—colors like gray, brown, or fawn—rather than the predominant, glaring white.

The Architecture of Country Houses reiterates the importance of "fitness" in buildings. Herein lies the essence of Downing's convictions. It was really not the Gothic or any other architectural style which obsessed him. His ideal was the function, the suitability, and the honesty of the design.

Phoebe Stanton has written about the church architecture of the period: "One enduring product of the Gothic Revival was the conviction that the architecture of an age illustrates its inner nature, strengths and weaknesses and that the architect may influence for good or bad, the lives of those around him. The second lasting contribution of the revival was its insistence that the function of a building should be expressed in its appearance. Expanded knowledge of the history of architecture had demonstrated that in buildings of quality and in periods of artistic creativity use had indeed been visible in and had directed design."* This was Downing's doctrine, applied to domestic architecture.

If the exteriors of Downing's designs were matters of gravity to him, he was equally concerned with the interiors of his dwellings. His floor plans provided clearly articulated spaces defined by their function. The entrance was typically set off by a wide porch or veranda which became one of the hallmarks of architecture of this period. One entered directly into a hall rather than into a living area in order "to protect the dignity and privacy" of the occupants. The kitchen and the living rooms were always on the ground floor, while the sleeping chambers were almost always on the second. For larger residences, Downing simply embellished the original plan, deepening the design to include extra rooms in back and above. Nor did he neglect the interior decoration in his houses. As always, he stressed the need to retain the original character of the structure and its purpose. Decoration as well as design was to be governed by principles of modesty and restraint.

Most of the architects who contributed plans to Downing's

*Phoebe Stanton, *The Gothic Revival and American Church Architecture* (Baltimore: Johns Hopkins University Press, 1968).

Alexander J. Davis, an 1852 portrait in watercolor by George Freeman.

books also produced their own pattern books. Among them were A.J. Davis's *Rural Residences* (1837), Gervase Wheeler's *Rural Homes* (1851), and Calvert Vaux's *Villas and Cottages* (1857).

They, too, emphasized the importance of natural materials in construction. An obvious choice was wood. Not only was there an incredible supply available, it was far less expensive than stone and easier to work with. New tools like the steam-powered scroll saw and the development of building methods such as balloon framing made wooden construction inevitable as the choice of the average home builder. Furthermore, a talented carpenter could provide variations of the intricate Gothic motifs. And to the rising middle class these were symbols of affluence. What the rich might originally have effected in stone, the common man could now mimic in a more modest material.

Paradoxically, the house pattern books provided the public with highly affordable and comfortable designs and, at the same time, the tempting opportunity to indulge in outrageous excesses. Downing had inveighed against "cottages . . . highly decorated with overwrought bargeboards on all the gables and an excess of fanciful and flowing ornaments of a cardboard character." Yet in many instances the simple gables and barge-boards of Downing's unpretentious cottages quickly became a veritable riot of decoration, carved in cheap, thin wood, engendering the term "gingerbread."

"Then came what is well called 'Carpenter Gothic,' marked by the same high indifference to structural integrity and with even less reliance on precedent for its architectural forms; a perfectly awful farrago of libellous details—pointed arches, clustered columns, buttresses, parapets, pinnacles. And with these awful monuments, cheek by jowl, Italian villas, very white and much balconied, Swiss chalets and every other imaginable thing. . .that the admirable Mr. Downing could invent, with for evidence of sterling American ingenuity, the 'jig-saw-batten' refinement of crime." So fumed American architect Ralph Adams Cram in an address before the Contemporary Club of Philadelphia. The address was later published in the July 1913 issue of *The Yale Review* as well as *The Architectural Record* of the same period.

Mr. Cram did Mr. Downing an injustice. (Downing,

himself, had sadly acknowledged that his countrymen seemed ready to try a new style every day.) But unwittingly Cram had made an interesting point. What was the origin of all these designs? The original Gothic drew on only a few and obvious sources—ecclesiastical or the forms of nature—the fir tree as a pointed Gothic arch, for example. In the machine-turned knobs and spindles there were also references to furniture designs, such as those of Charles Eastlake which were crisp and cleanly articulated. Beyond that, it was up to the imagination of the creator, or so it seems.

The Craftsmen and the Architects

Primitive scroll sawing, 1775.

In England the Gothic Revival had occurred on two levels. One was that of the craftsmen who perpetuated techniques and designs from the Middle Ages and passed these methods on from generation to generation, constituting "Gothic Survival." The other, beginning with the late eighteenth century, was that architects, too, became interested in Gothic through the romantic Picturesque movement. Walpole's controversial residence Strawberry Hill and Benjamin Henry Latrobe's Sedgeley built in 1799 in Philadelphia for William Crammond, as well as the writing of innovators like Pugin, further strengthened this interest.

The American Gothic Revival was also split between the work of architects, such as Ithiel Town and his partner A.J. Davis, and the construction of local carpenters who copied the designs in house pattern books. Davis, himself, worked on both levels, directly with his wealthy clients and broadly by publishing plans in house pattern books. Almost alone among his colleagues, he provided builders and clients alike with very detailed specification sheets for which he charged $50 to $100. The designs that American carpenters were using in this period were related to the Gothic Revival, as was any building which displayed tracery or ornamented bargeboards, even if the architectural style was Swiss chalet or Tuscan villa. There were no pattern books which contained precise instructions for producing Gothic buildings (as builders' guides had previously described the classical orders). So the builder had plenty of leeway.

The Wedding Cake House,
Kennebunkport, Maine.

Wood mortising machines: (top) 1807; (above) 1845.

Some of the most fascinating Carpenter Gothic designs resulted from the remodeling of much earlier buildings. In Calvert Vaux's *Villas and Cottages*, he shows three plates illustrating such a renovation that he and Downing did. In some cases, complete new facades were built over existing houses. Perhaps the most famous of these is the Wedding Cake House in Kennebunkport, Maine (see additional photographs of this house on pages 128-131). Beneath its decorations lies a prim Federal front. Carried away by the times and the erection of a Gothic barn adjacent to his house, the owner George W. Bourne designed and executed a rollicking new trim. Although it is not a pure example, this house has come to be regarded as the quintessence of Carpenter Gothic.

It is hard to believe that the appealing and light-hearted Carpenter Gothic ornamentation, which spread across the American landscape, actually evolved from such a somber aesthetic as the Gothic. And that the delicate filigree of leaf, vine, and inviting arch rose out of " . . . an architecture . . . peculiarly Christian . . . whose very ornaments remind one of the joy beyond the grave, whose lofty vaults and arches are crowded with the forms of prophets and martyrs and beatified spirits and seem to resound with the choral hymns of angels and archangels . . . the architecture of Christianity, the sublime, the glorious Gothic," as architectural critic Henry R. Cleveland declaimed in 1836.

Whatever myriad and whimsical forms its ornamentation took, Carpenter Gothic offers some of the finest examples of native American craftsmanship. Here, indeed, was the perfect blend of the inherent skills of the American carpenter and a new technology. The creators, mainly anonymous, have disappeared, but the delightful embroidery remains, infinitely more appealing and personal than today's structures of steel and glass.

Plates

William J. Rotch, Esq. House

Alexander Jackson Davis, architect
New Bedford, Massachusetts
Built 1846

This inherently elegant house is one of the most famous of its period. It was designed by Alexander Jackson Davis and built for William J. Rotch of New Bedford, Massachusetts. *The Architecture of Country Houses* printed a floor plan and showed a front elevation. It is Design **XXIV**: A Cottage-Villa in a Rural Gothic Style.

Here is Downing's own description: "The body of the house is nearly square and the elevation is a successful illustration of the manner in which a form, usually uninteresting, can be so treated as to be highly picturesque. There is, indeed, a combination of the aspiring lines of the roof with the horizontal lines of the veranda, which expresses picturesqueness and domesticity very successfully. The high pointed gable of the central and highest part of this design has a bold and spirited effect, which would be out of keeping with the cottage-like modesty of the drooping, hipped roof, were it not for the equally bold manner in which the chimneytops spring upwards. Altogether then, we should say that the character expressed by the exterior of this design is that of a man or family of domestic tastes, but with strong aspirations after something higher than social pleasures."

Mr. Rotch's father thought the plans for the house "disgusting," presumably because they were so unlike other New Bedford residences. But William J. Rotch prevailed, much to the pleasure of his descendants who still live there.

William J. Rotch, Esq. House

Athenwood

Thomas Waterman Wood, original owner
and probable designer
Montpelier, Vermont
Built 1850

When the twenty-six-year-old artist Thomas Waterman Wood took his bride Minerva Robertson home to his rural Gothic cottage, she must have been charmed. Wood, trained as a cabinetmaker, had designed it in anticipation of their marriage. A talented local carpenter, Franklyn Hoyt, is believed to have supervised its construction. No matter who deserves the credit, there is little doubt that inspiration for the cottage drew heavily on the current pattern books of that period.

With a board-and-batten exterior, the main block of the structure is essentially rectangular, although the enclosed entrance porch projects far enough to suggest a cruciform plan. Three large gables delineate the building's shape, but it is the overscaled, elaborate tulip leaf pattern on bargeboard and hood-mold which dominates the design. The main windows flanking the front door are 9 feet (2.74 m) high with diamond panes and ogee hood-molds, which give a distinctive arch to the windows. The ornamentation does not end there. A grape leaf and vine motif enlivens the eaves. Tucked beneath the gables are French doors, which open onto the roof. To some observers the effect seems almost Oriental.

Wood called his home "Athenwood"—combining the Greek version of his wife's first name and his surname. Until the 1880s Athenwood also served as his studio. Then he built a new one on the hill north of this house, tying the two dissimilar structures together with the intensive use of the same carved designs. Minerva died before him, but Wood spent his summers here until his death in 1903. Today Athenwood sets precipitously above a heavily trafficked street, its front yard sacrificed to widen the road. It is still a startling and enchanting sight.

Peter Davis House

Noank, Connecticut
Built 1852

Noank was the East Coast capital of the wooden shipbuilding trade when the four Davis brothers, James, Henry, Horace, and Peter, built their houses on Pearl Street above the harbor. All were sailors and, of necessity, had a sound knowledge of carpentry. However, it was Peter, the youngest, who was the best carpenter and who enhanced not only his own, but his brothers' houses with handsomely crafted ornamentation. When he built his own house in 1852, he was twenty-two years old and unmarried. Only when the house was finished did he seek a wife.

Essentially, the house is plain in mass and plan with its porch and chimney so expressive of home and security. It is his carving which makes this small house especially appealing. The repetition of the same forms on the gable, on the hood molds, and again pendant from the porch eaves is very satisfying. Similarly, the circular cutout at the top of the porch supports crowns the porch railing. Finally, the flowing leaf and vine design and the lovely, stylized lily, hanging inverted from the gable peak, are a sinuous and romantic counterpoint to the crispness of the other carving. A case has been made for the sexual symbolism of many carved designs of this period. One could speculate on this house.

James Hope House

James Hope, probable designer
Castleton, Vermont
Built c. 1850

The exquisite thistle and leaf ornamentation on this Castleton, Vermont, house is generally believed to be the design of its owner, the painter James Hope, who may have created it in memory of his birthplace. Born in Roxburgshire, Scotland, on November 29, 1818, he and his family emigrated to Canada while he was still a child. By the late 1840s he was teaching drawing and painting at the Castleton Seminary. He built his house and studio (not shown) about 1850.

Especially notable are the balcony railing, which repeats the thistle and leaf carving and the fluid, frond-like bracket under the balcony. Opening onto the balcony is a double-light Gothic arched window. A quatrefoil design in wood appears at the apex of the window. A careful look at the ell will show how the frond motif was carried through on the porch supports. (Unfortunately the house was under renovation when the picture was taken.)

Hope painted many pictures of Castleton and its environs, among them "Bird Mountain, Castleton, Vermont," which is in the M. & M. Karolik Collection at the Museum of Fine Arts in Boston, Massachusetts. It is dated 1855 and shows many recognizable houses in Castleton, including his own. The painting is signed directly beneath Hope's house, which was then painted yellow.

Courtesy Museum of Fine Arts, Boston.

James Monroe House

Guilford, Connecticut
Built 1850

In Guilford, Connecticut, renowned for its eighteenth-century houses, this Gothic house is a handsome anomaly. Built in 1850, it is a substantial dwelling which has been added on to over the years. For example, the second floor of the projecting wing is, very likely, an addition. The strong, supporting columns of the entrance portico suggest the builder was influenced by ecclesiastical design, as does the cruciform inscribed on the three wooden tablets atop the portico.

The house is painted charcoal gray and sheathed in the customary board-and-batten siding. The detail—such as the drip-stones—is less fanciful than in most houses of the period and conveys a stronger architectural feeling.

As an example of contemporary living in a house of this period, it is outstanding. The interior, furnished handsomely in a sparse and eclectic fashion, emphasizes the ceiling heights and makes the best of a number of small rooms. The carriage shed, with its quatrefoil window and simple, scalloped bargeboard, happily shatters the earth-tone concept of Downing Gothic. Remodeled into a spacious studio, it is painted grape color with a lovely explosion of orange pyracantha espaliered against it.

D. Flanders House

South Royalton, Vermont
Built 1864

No one stayed the skillful hand or flourishing imagination of the carpenter who built this house in the 1860s. Situated on a hill above the town of South Royalton, Vermont, the decoration has a spontaneity which evokes an immediate response. Except for the inverted wave pattern on the bargeboards and the hood molds over the door and windows, there is no similarity in the designs of the carving. Nevertheless, everything seems to work together, including the cutouts flanking the front door, which have a Pennsylvania Dutch flavor. The basic architectural plan probably came from a house pattern book. If so, the plan was enhanced by the talents of a master carpenter.

John J. Brown House

Henry Rowe, architect
Portland, Maine
Built 1845

Not only is the John J. Brown House the earliest example of Gothic Revival in Portland, Maine, it is also one of the earliest in the state. It was designed by Henry Rowe, an Irish-born, English-trained architect, who emigrated to the United States in 1840 and moved to Portland five years later. Although he was apparently prolific, this is the only house that is absolutely documented as his.

An ardent disciple of the Gothic, he advertised in the *Portland Reference Book and City Directory* for 1846 that he "could supply gentlemen with plans, elevations, sections and details of buildings in every style from the most elaborate Gothic to the most simple and unadorned, on the most reasonable terms."

Rowe worked in New York and Boston before moving to Portland and was undoubtedly familiar with Downing and other contemporaries. In fact, it is possible that this cottage was also based on Design II in *Cottage Residences* (see pages 15, 84). If so, Rowe adapted the design to his own purpose, discarding among other things flanking porches and a pinnacle, tightening the overall plan, and adding his own ideas, such as the angled buttresses. The result is an elegant, small townhouse with a disarming medieval feel.

House

Chester, Vermont
Built c. 1870-1880

Elements of Queen Anne (the great pedimented gable, the octagonal and curved towers) and Eastlake (the crisp, machine-turned spindles and knobs) combine exuberantly in this Chester, Vermont, house. This galaxy of Carpenter Gothic effects is a delightful example of what the word "gingerbread" conveys to most people. Although no date is available on the house, it was probably built between 1870 and 1880.

Roseland

Henry Bowen, original owner
Joseph Collins Wells, architect
Woodstock, Connecticut
Built 1846

Architect Joseph Collins Wells who designed this beautiful Gothic villa was also the designer of one of the first wooden Gothic houses in America (see pages 98-103). English-born and educated, he must have been weaned on Gothic tradition.

Built in 1846 as a country retreat for wealthy silk merchant Henry Bowen, Roseland (so-called because of its gardens) has a far reaching view. And in those days, Bowen was the master of much he surveyed. He was a sixth-generation Bowen in Woodstock, had clerked for a while in his father's general store, then left for a more promising job in New York City. He became a successful businessman and later was publisher and sole owner of the influential Congregational journal, *Independent*. (Two of his editors were the Reverend Henry Beecher Stowe and Theodore Tilton, and Bowen became embroiled in the scandalous lawsuit between the two men.)

It is fascinating to envision the once vibrant life at Roseland. Four United States presidents were guests here, and Bowen, as *paterfamilias* in his hometown, invited many prominent and talented people to visit. Today this impressive house looks much as it did then, although the porte-cochère may have been added in the 1880s. The heavy carving on the bargeboards, the projecting pavilion with its Gothic windows, the triple gables, and clustered polygonal chimney stacks all combine to give weight and dignity to the essentially rectangular house.

44

Cottage

Exeter, New Hampshire
Built c. 1840s

This winning cottage on the Common in Exeter, New Hampshire, is one of the few houses of this vintage in the state which seems right out of a house pattern book without any major eclectic variations. With its flush-boarded exterior, smartly molded and pierced bargeboards, and big windows, it commands instant attention. Now painted the sparkling white that Downing so disliked, it was once a drabber, "natural" hue. The present owner, an architect, found the original paint color under the existing white and wants to repaint it in those tones. Although he and his family prefer a contemporary interior, his respect for the historic traditions of the house has led him into research on the period and an application for an Historic Landmarks designation.

Townsend House

Windsor, Vermont
Built c. 1847

When Isaac Townsend, a clock-maker, died in 1812, he left all his property to his widow, Sarah. Sarah sold much of her inheritance but kept a choice lot near the Windsor Common. There, in late 1847 or early 1848 she built herself a fashionable Gothic Revival cottage. Unkind relatives said that it cost so much, she couldn't afford to live in it. She did not really get the chance since she

the work of Clark Cabot who designed the Boston Atheneum.

Through the years the house was sold to several families. Certain features, such as the flared roof over the front porch and the layering of shingles (instead of board and batten), suggest at least one owner succumbed to the temptation of further embellishment in the Queen Anne style. Nevertheless, this lacy valentine—still

died in 1848. The tax list for that year records that the "Widow I. Townsend" was assessed for a new house "valued at $1,200." No one knows whether the original plan was from a house pattern book or

enjoyed as a private residence—is enchanting and holds its own in a neighborhood of staunch early American and later Victorian structures, including a Richardsonian neighbor.

Cottage

Madison, Connecticut
Built 1873

This gray cottage located on a street not far from Long Island Sound is, at first glance, pattern book perfect. The familiar vertical sheathing, ornamented bargeboards, and comfortable shady porch are all specifications of the 1840-1850 design books. The porch supports, however, indicate that the house was built at a later date—and town records bear this out. It was constructed in 1873, and according to a neighborhood historian, some additional ornamentation was added in the early 1900s. It is a fine example of how the Carpenter Gothic influence endured long after its heyday. In a town with over 125 houses built before 1800, this is the only one of this type which still exists in an instantly recognizable form.

House

William Fenno Pratt,
probable designer
Northampton, Massachusetts
Built 1840

This charming, small house with its steep gable is deceptively simple in its adornment. The builder (quite possibly William Fenno Pratt) drew on the horticultural sources, so dear to the period, and the results are joyful. The roof brackets, like the branches of trees, seem to flow out of the board-and-batten siding. The supports of the small porch also seem to rise naturally, leading the eye to the roof and the plain cutout designs under its eaves. This building was once a gardener's cottage and part of a large estate. Today it is a staff residence for a private school.

Two Houses

Jacob Chickering, builder
Andover, Massachusetts
Built c. 1840

With the tremendous expansion of the textile mills and the subsequent need for employee housing, Andover, Massachusetts, was aswarm with excellent carpenters in the 1840s. Moses Clement, Levi Farnham, Samuel Moor, John H. Perry, and William Spiller are among the many whose names and building activities have been surprisingly well preserved. Of them all, however, Jacob Chickering was the best known and documented.

The North Andover Historical Society owns 113 of Chickering's business papers. Housed at the Merrimack Valley Textile Museum, they include miscellaneous, uncataloged bills, building estimates, and receipts for the years 1834-1878. As a carpenter, Chickering worked in partnership with Nathaniel Whittier. Over the years he progressed from carpenter to contractor until eventually he opened a shop to make pianos. (This was the forerunner of the Chickering piano company.)

Chickering built houses of all kinds, including Greek Revival, but seemed to find a happy niche in the Gothic idiom. Here are two of his houses, which at a quick glance might seem identical. They display Chickering's feel for delightful tracery which is not overdone. The birdlike cutout on one and the crenellations capping the bay window and portico roof on the other are not flimsy in any sense. Both houses have a very substantial look and sit well on their sites: one behind a handsome fence, the other on the brow of a hill.

House, Andover, Massachusetts

Wetmore-Weeks House

Middletown, Connecticut
Built c. 1755

The Wetmore-Weeks House is a Wesleyan University campus landmark, long believed to have been built in 1755 by a member of the wealthy Wetmore family. New research indicates that this Middletown, Connecticut, residence may have belonged instead to another well-to-do citizen, Jabez Hamlin. There are no problems, however, concerning the identity of the man who bought it in 1839. He was Charles Alsop, and it does not take a clairvoyant to notice that he succumbed to the spell of the Gothic Revival. In fact while remodeling took place, he leased the house behind this one for three years, presumably to stay out of the carpenters' way. Almost every Victorian fancy is illustrated here, including ornamented bargeboards, finials, diamond-paned windows, clustered, corbelled brick chimneys, and layered shingles. The photograph of the house in the snow shows it as it was before receiving a coat of dark brown paint. The trim, newly highlighted by the paint, makes the tracery seem very like that of The Stone Cottage (see pages 78-79). It is quite possible the same carpenter cut out the ornamentation on both.

Wetmore-Weeks House

George A. Pillsbury House

Concord, New Hampshire
Built 1864

There is no doubt that the builder of this house had an extensive architectural vocabulary, although he missed a lot in the translation. Built in 1864, the overall form and proportions as well as the corner pilasters are Federal or late Colonial. There are also elements of Greek Revival, Italianate, and Gothic Revival style. For example, the drip hood moldings are Gothic, the cornice brackets Italianate, and the pedimented, center pavilion Greek Revival. Even so, the house has a definite feeling of being well-built and, despite its mélange of periods, projects a comfortable and comforting, bourgeois image.

John Adams House

Worthington, Massachusetts
Built 1848

This house was built in 1848 by John Adams, who was a distant cousin of Downing's. (Downing married Caroline DeWindt, the great niece of John Quincy Adams.) The rumor persists that the house was designed by Downing. (Despite his kinship to Adams, this seems highly unlikely.) If he did, it was a one-of-a-kind design. This house has a strong ecclesiastical flavor, with its steep piers and the small second-story canopied balcony which seems like a pulpit. When seen from a distance through trees, its country setting somewhat softens the severity of the design.

John Adams House

A Small Cottage for a Working Man

Design I from *The Architecture of Country Houses*

This is the simplest of Downing's designs and is appropriately Design I. In his era, it could be constructed for $330 or $400. This is how he described it: "Let anyone imagine this little cottage with its roof cut off close to the eaves, with the rafter brackets that support the projecting eaves omitted, with the windows and door mere bare frames and he has an example of how this same cottage would look as we commonly see it built; that is to say, without the picturesqueness of wood clearly expressed by using it boldly (not neatly and carefully): by a sense of something beyond mere utility, evinced in the pains taken to extend the roof more than is absolutely needful; and by raising the character of the windows and doors by placing hoods over their tops."

James A. Latham House

Noank, Connecticut
Built 1853

This board-and-batten house was built in 1853 in Noank, Connecticut, for James Latham. It obviously drew on Downing's design for a workingman's cottage (see opposite page) as well as other of his schemes. Its proportions, broad rather than vertical, are the builder's own idea. The detail, however, is exactly as Downing ordered—the hood molds over the windows and doors and the loop of tracery on the raking board of the projecting gable give distinction to the simplest of houses.

House

Castleton, Vermont
Built c. 1850

Known locally as the "Old Music Academy," this building was once the Elmwood Institute, a select boarding school for young ladies constructed about 1850. The principal, Reverend Pease, was a retired minister. His calling may have had architectural significance, in this particular instance, for the dominant element of this structure is its windows, adapted from an obviously ecclesiastical source—the beautiful Gothic arch of so many churches. Unlike its neighbor down the street, the James Hope House, this design is too austere for elaborate tracery. Yet the sharp verticality of its windows and the crisp details, such as the labels and tilted sills, make it a compelling structure. The Old Music Academy, now a private residence, shows how varied the expression of Carpenter Gothic was.

Justin Smith Morrill Homestead

Justin Smith Morrill, original owner
and probable designer
Strafford, Vermont
Built 1848-1851

It is fitting that the Justin Morrill Homestead in Strafford, Vermont, should have a park-like setting with old trees, a lively brook, and open land around it. Morrill, a United States Senator from Vermont, fathered the Land-Grant College Bill which became law under President Lincoln in 1862. All his long life (1810-1898) Morrill loved farming and the land. He was a self-made man, prosperous enough to retire at age thirty-eight, who also loved reading. After his retirement, he devoted much of his time to these two interests and his family.

His house was begun in 1848 and the design is said to have been his own. He was a romantic—a true man of his time—and a devotee of Sir Walter Scott's novels (as was A.J. Davis). So it is possible that he consulted standard pattern books and embellished the plans with details from his own fantasies. The exact origin of the design seems unimportant when one looks at this charming, flush-boarded cottage, with its paint ombred a pale rose-beige to resemble weathered stone. The exquisite carving of the wooden cusped tracery around the exterior of the din-ing room window, the fanciful bargeboards like icicles hanging from the gables, and all the other picturesque touches are enchanting.

The house was finished in 1851, and Morrill brought his bride of a few months to live there. Her name was Ruth Swan and she was from Easton, Massachusetts, adjacent to North Easton. It would be nice to think that at some point on a return visit to her hometown, they saw that other Gothic cottage, Queset (see pages 74-75), the home of Oakes Angier Ames, finished only three years later.

Justin Smith Morrill Homestead

Hopkins House

Northampton, Massachusetts
Built c. 1850-1860

Confusion surrounds the original owner and the date of construction of this flush-boarded villa, now a dormitory at Smith College in Northampton, Massachusetts. Once believed to have been commissioned by Lafayette Maltby, a local banker, it has been owned by Smith since 1924. Its mansard roof is suggestive of French Empire, but in any terms, it is a freely expressed, romantic house whose Gothic emphasis is not dependent on tracery. For its period it is a very conservative design.

Commodore Charles Green House

South Windsor, Connecticut
Built 1851

This charming sixteen-room Gothic cottage, situated on almost 20 acres in South Windsor, Connecticut, was completed in 1851 for Commodore Charles Green. His descendants lived there for 100 years. The present owners bought the house in 1961 and, aside from making necessary repairs and decorating the interior, made no structural changes. They believe the house to have been an A.J. Davis design. If so, Commodore Green obviously drew from many other sources, as well, to answer his own needs. There are some unusual details—clustered chimney stacks with an almost medieval buttress, the oversized gable, the steeply pitched roof, and the crenellations at the porch roof line, which are quite military in feeling.

Gaylord-Bassett Villa

William Gaylord, original owner
Northampton, Massachusetts
Built 1851

This unusual house was built for an iron manufacturer, William Gaylord. Despite its name, "Gaylord-Bassett Villa," it bears a striking similarity to Design XVIII in *The Architecture of Country Houses*: A Bracketed American Farmhouse. The total effect is very vertical. Automatically the eye travels upward toward the thrust of the roof brackets and the trim, which rises straight up from the roof as if jolted by electricity. The setting is now suburban, but originally the gardens were laid out to enjoy a long view of the Mount Holyoke range of mountains.

Queset

Oakes Angier Ames,
original owner
North Easton, Massachusetts
Built 1854

In its fusion of architectural design and harmonious landscape, this beautiful house represents Downing philosophy and Davis talent at their most felicitous. However, this is only a pretty supposition. Downing had been dead for two years by the time it was constructed, and all plans pertaining to it have been lost or destroyed. Nor does it show up anywhere in the voluminous papers left by Davis. Nevertheless, the "fitness and suitability" and all those other beloved ideals are here.

It was built in 1854 for a rich manufacturer, Oakes Angier Ames. Its rusticated stone construction points to a local tradition of masonry, borne out in later years when North Easton became a bastion of Richardson romanesque design. Sometime in the 1880s, the garden was added; it is attributed to Frederick Law Olmsted.

Almost nothing of the interior is original, but the main block with its symmetrical front and the broken up garden façade, remains virtually the same. The clustered colonettes and wooden ornamentation are simple and appropriate to the stone construction. Whoever the architect was, he dealt sensitively with the house. To see this handsome structure set with such ease in the New England countryside is an enthralling experience.

Deacon Merrill C. Dodge House

Greenville, New Hampshire
Built 1850

There is little documentation on this house in Greenville, New Hampshire, except that it was built for Deacon Merrill C. Dodge in 1850. The carpenter who built the Dodge House seems to have been intrigued with the play of shadow as a means of enhancing design. To this end he placed a flat board behind the trim at the porch level, so the shadows of the trim would be reflected more dramatically.

The Stone Cottage

Edward Duane Barnes, original owner
and probable designer
Middletown, Connecticut
Built 1846

Edward Duane Barnes was an important Middletown, Connecticut, businessman and, according to contemporary reports, a leader of the literary avant garde in the town. He was also very interested in building and in 1846 designed The Stone Cottage for his own residence. Although once thought to be a Davis plan, recent research points to it as Barnes' own. (This does not necessarily signify wild originality, since even the outstanding professionals of the period borrowed freely from one another.) In anyone's terms, however, the house is a very successful venture and exhibits a real affinity with the architectural idiom of the period.

The house is stone—probably from the nearby Portland quarries. The ornamentation of wood is extraordinarily beautiful, suggestive of medieval manuscript illumination. The trim is executed with such precision that it includes the casements of the cellar windows.

Today The Stone Cottage is the infirmary for Wesleyan University.

Alvah Littlefield Cottage

William Fenno Pratt, designer
Northampton, Massachusetts
Built 1864

On March 29, 1859, the *Daily Hampshire Gazette* reported: "Dr. A. Littlefield of Boston is building a beautiful summer residence on Bridge Street, near Mr. Humphrey's, after a plan drawn by Mr. Pratt." William Fenno Pratt was a leading builder in tne area, and many of his houses still stand in Northampton (see pages 50-51 for another of Pratt's designs).

The Littlefield Cottage was one of a group of three Gothic cottages on Bridge Street and was considered the most ornate. Despite its run-down appearance and ungainly changes in the roof, it still has some charming touches. But Bridge Street abuts a major thruway, and the future of this little house seems uncertain, at best.

A Small Bracketed Cottage

Design II from *The Architecture of Country Houses*

No matter how elementary the design, Downing always tried to allow for some extra measurement of comfort and style. This is demonstrated in his description of A Small Bracketed Cottage: Design II, which in his time cost $512.00 to construct. He wrote: "The little rustic arbors or covered seats on the outside of the bay window may be supposed to answer in some measure in the place of a veranda and convey, at first glance, an expression of refinement and taste attained in that simple manner so appropriate to a small cottage."

Homer Swift House

Milford, Connecticut
Built 1865

Design II in *The Architecture of Country Houses*: A Small Bracketed Cottage (see page 82) was the model for a Connecticut flour miller, Homer Swift, when he built his house in 1865. The only extra flourish he gave it was the hood molds over the windows and door. The exterior remains essentially the same except for the obvious additions of the concrete porch and modern iron railings. The interior, also very simple and adhering to the original floor plan, remains essentially unspoiled. Even the well house is original except for the louvered blinds—a protection against modern-day vandals.

Henry Mason Brooks House

Salem, Massachusetts
Built 1851

Painted a resounding green and accented with white, this dramatic villa stops traffic on Salem's hectic Lafayette Street. Copied from Design II of Andrew Jackson Downing's *Cottage Residences* (shown on the left), it was built for Henry Mason Brooks, a local businessman. Mr. Brooks, who was born, educated, and died in Salem, was a scholarly, old-fashioned gentleman who had the means to pursue the collecting of rare books and coins. He also wrote on many aspects of Salem history.

To judge from his residence, he was as *au courant* with the present as the past. This is a marvelous example of the period, and the white paint picks up the architectural points of the house in startling detail. What look like finials above the porch roof are actually trompe l'oeil echoing the finial at the peak of the central gable. It is possible that some wooden trim has fallen off, and the paint was a simple expedient.

The Kibbe House

Somers, Connecticut
Built c. 1843

Except for its verticality, this plain, unembellished house is a cross between Downing's Design I: A Workingman's Cottage (see page 62) and Design II: A Small Bracketed Cottage (see page 82). Freely adapted as these designs usually were, it is impossible to tell whether the fluted Doric columns with scroll brackets which support the porch roof were original with the house. If they were, they were all wrong for the purists of the period but apparently just what the builder wanted.

Reverend Edward Hall House

Alfred Stone, architect
Providence, Rhode Island
Built c. 1864

On College Hill in Providence, Rhode Island, this house built about 1864 sits somber and heavy amid some glorious brick mansions. Although it is called the Reverend Edward Hall House, it was actually built by his widow after his death. It is a transitional house, employing some Gothic elements, but simpler and larger than many of the period and perhaps hampered by its direct access to the street. The house was designed by Alfred Stone, a then relatively unknown architect who moved to Providence from Maine in 1864. He prospered and by the late 1800s was the senior partner in one of Providence's most prestigious architectural firms, Stone, Carpenter, Willson.

Kingscote

George Noble Jones, original owner
Richard Upjohn, architect
Newport, Rhode Island
Built 1839

In 1839 when Richard Upjohn designed this handsome villa for the George Noble Jones family of Savannah, Georgia, there were no reproduction marble palaces on Newport's Bellevue Avenue. So for a while at least, nothing stood between the house and the sea. The Jones family lived there summers until the advent of the Civil War. Presumably, to avoid its confiscation, they deeded the property to a Canadian relative and went home to Savannah.

In 1864 the house was acquired by William Henry King, who named it Kingscote. Some years earlier, in 1845, Upjohn had done "A Villa in the Italian Style" for King's brother Edward. It stood directly behind the Noble Jones house and is Design XXVIII in *The Architecture of Country Houses.* Both King brothers had been in the East Indian trade from

their teens when their father bought them places with the noted firm of Russell & Company in Boston. Russell & Company's primary interest was not the treasures of the Orient but opium. The King brothers amassed fortunes and retired in their twenties. Edward was about thirty-four years old when he moved into Kingscote. His happiness there was short-lived. In 1870 he went mad and spent the remaining forty-five years of his life in an asylum. As befitted a gentleman, he occupied a suite, employed a valet, kept his own carriage, and imported his cigars.

The property was left to King's great-niece, Gwendolyn Ella Rives, who lived there until 1972. When she died, she left the house to the Preservation Society of Newport County with an endowment to maintain it. Except for a three story wing by Stanford White, which was added in 1881 and includes a sumptuous dining room, the house remains structurally the same as Upjohn planned it. Unlike his charming interiors, his exterior design is bold and severe. (Surprisingly, the same size hood-molds are used over the interior doors.) The trim on Kingscote is simple, almost understated, and has a pleasing unity. The original paint color on the house was a creamy buff, and trumpet vines, honeysuckle, and other plantings

were used abundantly to soften the exterior lines. The battleship gray color, which makes the wooden structure look like a fortress of impregnable stone, came with the 1881 addition.

The interior of Kingscote is a mélange of wonderful things—Louis Tiffany tiles and stained glass, French furniture, old silver, Chinese Export china, some good American furniture, and sentimental memorabilia. All of it is a reminder of the two owners who left under tragic circumstances and never returned.

Downing House

Andover, Massachusetts
Built 1840

To the best of anyone's knowledge this house in Andover, Massachusetts, was built for a Boston businessman named Downing as his summer home. Andover was very rural then and the house was set in an orchard. There is no record concerning the builder, which is unusual in the Andover area. The present owners love it, maintain it beautifully and feel most of the design is original. If so, the builder used his own free-wheeling interpretation of the current architectural mode. It doesn't matter. It is a most attractive house.

A Lake or River Villa for a Picturesque Site (Exterior)

Design XXXII from *The Architecture of Country Houses*

Design XXXII may have inspired the builder of the William Goodwin House (see pages 96-97) in Portland, Maine.

A Lake or River Villa for a
Picturesque Site (First Floor Plan)

Design **XXXII** from *The Architecture of Country Houses*

If Downing's inspirations for his picturesque exteriors were frequently romantic, foreign villas, his interior floor plans were almost always based on the practical living needs of the occupants. The first floor plan of Design **XXXII** is a very good one even in contemporary terms, if one could afford to build it today. The traffic flow is excellent, with all main rooms opening off a central hall. The rooms are spacious and private, with sliding doors to shut off each room. Thrown open, *en suite*, as Downing put it, the entry hall, library, drawing room, and dining room comprise 1,928 square feet of living space.

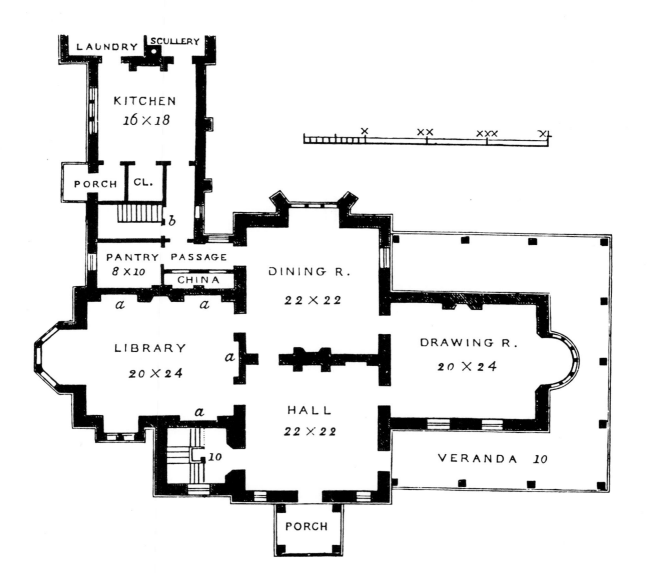

William A. Goodwin House

William A. Goodwin,
possible designer
Portland, Maine
Built 1859

The only established facts about this house are that it was built in 1859 by a civil engineer named William A. Goodwin. It could well be that in his profession Goodwin had a knowledge of pattern books and designed his own house. Whether he did or not, he certainly picked a handsome site for it on Portland's Western Promenade high above the Fore River. The location as well as striking architectural similarities makes one wonder if Goodwin's house was based on Design XXXII in *The Architecture of Country Houses*: A Lake or River Villa for a Picturesque Site (see pages 94-95).

Downing was in his element describing this house and its site because he was really describing the Hudson River Highlands which he loved so much and where he himself lived. "But let another person, gifted not only with common sense but imagination, live amid such scenery as meets his eye daily . . . and he will often feel that a common-place, matter-of-fact square house is an insult to the spirit of all that surrounds him. In such bold scenery, nature overpowers all and suggests all. . . . It is such picturesque scenery as this—scenery which exists in many spots in America besides the banks of the Hudson . . . it is there that the highly picturesque country house or villa is instinctively felt to harmonize

and belong to the landscape. It is there that the high tower, the steep roof and the boldly varied outline seem wholly in keeping with the landscape, because these forms in the building harmonize, either by contrast or assimilation with the pervading spirit of mysterious powers and beauty in romantic scenery."

It is obvious that Rhine River and Italian Lake villas were an influence on Design XXXII, and Downing freely admitted it. "[But] the general spirit of the composition is pointed without being strictly Gothic, and we have sought to produce effect by light and shade rather than intricate details. . . . Not to be wearisome regarding our river villa, we would add that we hope the reader will find in it the variety, independence and force of character, strong aspirations, and equally strong attachment to home and domestic life."

As happened most of the time when independent builders adapted Downing's designs to their own purposes, changes were made. For example, in the Goodwin House (assuming this is Design XXXII), the tower was not so high as portrayed in the etching, and it was built to the side of the house rather than in front. Although Goodwin placed his residence several blocks away from the river, it is quite possible that in his day the view was sweeping, obstructed only by a small cemetery.

The Cottage

Jonathan Sturges, original owner
Joseph Collins Wells, architect
Fairfield, Connecticut
Built 1840

These drawings and photographs of The Cottage in Fairfield, Connecticut, present an intriguing, 137-year-old history of a house and a family. The delicate rendering of the original plan and elevations was done by its architect, Joseph Collins Wells. As the plan shows, the house was spacious and comfortable with drawing room, dining room, and other common rooms on the ground floor and six bedrooms with bathing room on the second.

Meant for casual living, it was still well-built and some interesting features were employed in its construction. For example, an insulating layer of sand was used between the ground floor boards and the basement ceiling.

By the time the pen and ink sketch was done in 1972, the house had proliferated to 35 rooms, 11 staircases, 13 fireplaces, and (if you count the booktower) 6 stories. Front views of The Cottage are

obscured by wisteria and other foliage, but a side view of the eastern end of the house and details give a good indication of the strength of the design. As the additions kept pace with a large Victorian family, the exterior style maintained the proper tone.

The Cottage was commissioned in 1840 as a summer house by Jonathan Sturges, a prominent member of the New York financial community. One of the organizers of the Illinois Central Railroad, he also started the Bank of Commerce in Manhattan and was a founder and president of the Union League Club. Since then six generations have occupied the house and still do. Unlike Roseland (see pages 44-45), also designed by Wells, much is known about life at The Cottage. Its renowned collection of Hudson River Valley School paintings and first editions has been shared among the family for generations. Although some of the collection has been sold, enough remains for a small museum. Recently, a vigorous rehabilitation program has been undertaken on both house and property. Flower beds, long dormant, have been exhumed, and in one instance, 70 feet (21.3 m) of lumber were specially milled to replace trim at the rear of the house.

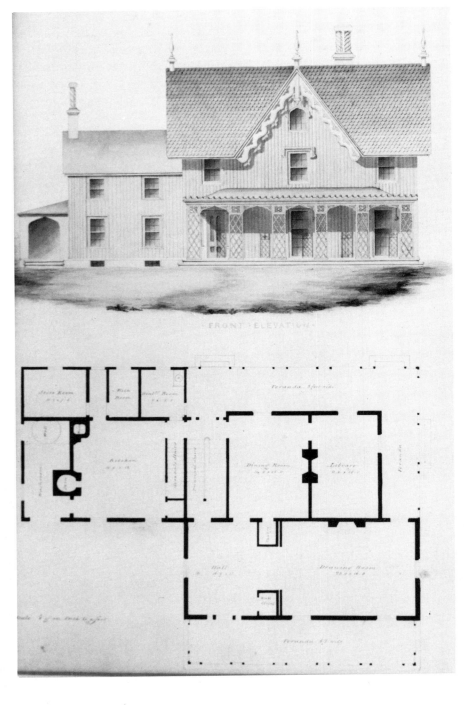

House

Peterborough, New Hampshire
Built c. 1845

This house in Peterborough,
New Hampshire, is said to have
been based on Design XXIV in
*The Architecture of Country
Houses.* If so, there were a lot
of changes made. The chunky
ornamentation illustrates how
effectively shadow can be used
as design in Carpenter Gothic.

House

East Haddam, Massachusetts
Built 1870

Little is known about the background of this Connecticut River Valley house. The town hall records trace the land sale back to 1870, but since the price of $3,000 for a quarter acre of land would have been very high then, it is probable that the house was already built and was included in the price.

Whatever its origin, the design is good, dominated by a huge gable which the rest of the exterior details do not fight. The graceful, welcoming curves of the porch openings and the clearly articulated leaf and flower ornamentation combine for a charming, picturesque effect.

Buttonwood Farm

The Adams Family, original owners
Chester, Vermont
Built 1880s

If there were ever a veranda which awakened visions of languid ladies in summer dimity and ice cold pitchers of claret lemonade, here it is. Like the mythical *mise-en-scène*, Buttonwood Farm no longer exists. It burned in 1964 and was never rebuilt. This impressive residence started life as a simple farmhouse on an 850-acre dairy farm in Chester, Vermont.

Sometime in the 1880s, the marvelous ornamentation was added to its austere façade. The son of the original owner lived at Buttonwood from his birth in 1898 until 1951. The house looked the same as long as he could remember. Even the long, dark shadows of winter only enhance the beauty of the design.

Henry Boody House

Gervase Wheeler, architect
Brunswick, Maine
Built 1849

In his *Rural Homes* Gervase Wheeler suggested as a "matin and even song to every architect and amateur, Mr. Ruskin's great maxim, 'Until common sense finds its way into architecture there can be but little hope for it. . . . '"

Wheeler practiced what he preached. Nowhere is this better demonstrated than in his plan for the Henry Boody House in Brunswick, Maine. The design was later published in *The Architecture of Country Houses* and described this way:

"This is essentially real. Its character is given by simplicity and fitness of construction. . . . The construction itself though simple is somewhat peculiar. It is framed but in such a manner as that on the exterior the construction shows and gives additional richness and character to the composition.

"At the corners are heavy posts, roughly dressed and champfered, and into them are mortised horizontal ties, immediately under the springing of the roof; these with the posts, and the studs, and framing of the roof, showing externally."

Young Henry Boody was a teacher of rhetoric at Bowdoin College in Brunswick when he commissioned the house. His account of the transaction has a very contemporary ring. He was quoted a price of $2,500 to build the house, although by the time the design was printed

by Downing three years later, the cost had risen to $2,800.

In March of 1850 Boody wrote his mother: "Enclosed I send you five dollars which you have wanted ere this and which I would have sent you had it been possible. You may perhaps wonder very much that with a salary of $1,000, I am so pinched for money but I can explain the whole mystery in few words. Last year I built a house which I expected would cost me $2,500. It actually cost me $5,000, independent of the land for which I paid $1,000.

This money I was obliged to hire at a very high rate of interest." Then Henry spelled it out in depressing, round sums:

To pay interest on borrowed money	$300
For fuel	150
For taxes	48
For insurance	40

By 1870 Boody had abandoned academe and his house for a richly rewarding life in New York as a banker and railroad president. There was a succession of owners after that. Since 1958 it has been the official residence of the Dean of Bowdoin College.

It is a charming place, with high ceilings and an airy feeling of open space one does not associate with the period. Surprisingly, there have been few interior changes except for two bedrooms and modern conveniences. The exterior color—a subtle sand tone—is the same as the first coat of paint, which was mixed with actual sand to resemble weathered stone. The sureness of the design and the handsome trim demonstrate the architect's skill in his medium.

Stephen Colton House

Longmeadow, Massachusetts
Built 1850

Essentially, this house built for Stephen Colton of Longmeadow, Massachusetts, in 1850 is a traditional rectangular house. Only the punched tracery and other delicate scrollwork mark it as a Gothic Revival house. Whoever the carpenter was, his restraint was admirable. He was able to achieve many Carpenter Gothic effects, working with very little but skillfully including the play of light and shadow in the ornamentation.

House

Granville, Massachusetts
Built 1850

On May 12, 1850, the sill for
this small board-and-batten cottage was laid by Silas Noble.
Utterly charming in its simplicity, this small house has
served for many years as the
summer home of one family.
They were so determined to
keep it unspoiled they did not
even wire it for electricity until
the 1940s. The porch with its
Doric columns was probably
added on late in the nineteenth
century.

Henry Thompson House

Thompsonville, Connecticut
Built c. 1845

The date of this house is in question, but there is no doubt that it was built for a wealthy carpet manufacturer, Henry Thompson, whose brother Orrin founded the town of Thompsonville and gave it the family name. The present owners bought it fifty-three years ago. They added plumbing and heating and changed a few windows. Otherwise, the house exterior looks much as it did in Henry Thompson's day.

Despite the modern touches, the owners have scrupulously maintained it. This is an important point. One reason many of these houses were torn down or drastically remodeled over the years is the high cost of maintenance. The present owners remember paying $5 to replace a tiny piece of interior wooden molding over fifty years ago, then a large price. Painted a rich, dark blue with white trim, this sixteen-room house, with its beautifully manicured shrubbery, is a compelling sight.

Henry Thompson House

House

Henry Austin, architect
Connecticut
Built 1878

If peals of organ music rolled out of this marvelous house, it would not seem extraordinary. Situated on a hill high above Long Island Sound, its ecclesiastical origin is immediately apparent. Nave, aisles, tower are all there along with the typical massing of Victorian churches. Even its exaggerated verticality seems to be reaching toward heaven. This is the late work of the noted architect Henry Austin, and it was built in 1878 at a time when most domestic designs were generally being executed by his associate David Brown. With its curved brackets, turned posts, and terrific play of light and shadow, this house is a most dramatic sight.

House, Connecticut

Cottage

Rockport, Massachusetts
Built 1870

A yellow and white candy box, if there ever was one, this cottage was built as a summer residence in Rockport, Massachusetts, for two brothers. It was originally board and batten, and some of the original siding still remains hidden under the clapboards.

When the current owner bought the property, it was in poor condition, and he practically took the house apart and put it back together again. Among other things he replaced fifty pieces of trim. Between his carpenter and himself, they turned out about three pieces an hour, using a router to cut the trim. (A router is a tool with a fine shaving bit which rotates—a kind of rotary plane.)

Whoever the builder was, he certainly understood the interplay of shadow and light created by the trim. To push the effect one step further, he nailed additional layers of ornamentation to the porch columns. The result is totally beguiling.

David Sikes House

Suffield, Connecticut
Built 1830s

This charming Gothic cottage is being restored by the descendants of the first owner, including his great-great grandson. Set in the middle of 40 acres in a rural Connecticut community, the house had been rented for a number of years until a disastrous fire made it uninhabitable. The family had two alternatives—to demolish it or restore it—they decided it was "too pretty to tear down." One interesting note: in order to replace the missing trim exactly, the great-great grandson made cardboard patterns to match the designs and cut them out with a carpenter's skill saw.

David Sikes House

The Wedding Cake House

Kennebunkport, Maine
Built c. 1820

Viewed from a certain angle, the Wedding Cake House (constructed as a proper brick Federal) looks as if it has been slipcovered in lace. It is undoubtedly the most famous example of Carpenter Gothic in New England and, to the thousands of tourists who have seen it, an absolute joy.

The Bryant Homestead

Ebenezer Snell, builder
Cummington, Massachusetts
Built 1785

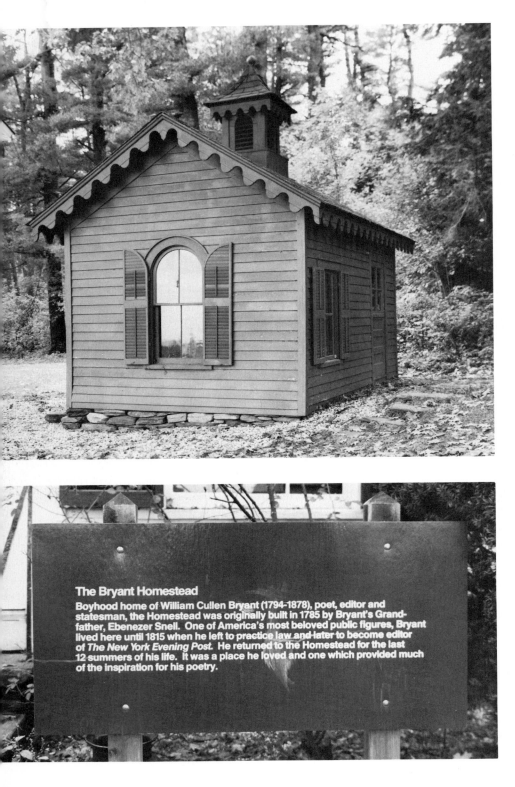

The Bryant Homestead

Boyhood home of William Cullen Bryant (1794-1878), poet, editor and statesman, the Homestead was originally built in 1785 by Bryant's Grandfather, Ebenezer Snell. One of America's most beloved public figures, Bryant lived here until 1815 when he left to practice law and later to become editor of *The New York Evening Post*. He returned to the Homestead for the last 12 summers of his life. It was a place he loved and one which provided much of the inspiration for his poetry.

This house, the family homestead of William Cullen Bryant, was built in 1785 by his grandfather Ebenezer Snell and enlarged over the years. Except for the little outbuilding with its simple Gothic trim, the house has little connection with Carpenter Gothic. But Bryant was one of the great cultural figures of the early nineteenth century and as such it is fascinating to see the house he loved more than any other. Here he spent his boyhood as well as the last twelve summers of his life.

House

Clinton, Connecticut
Built 1787

As the historical designation on this house confirms, it was built in 1787. Nothing is recorded about the enterprising carpenter who convinced the owner he should catch up with the times and go Gothic. On Clinton's main street, it is one of many eighteenth-century houses which capitulated to fashion. It is difficult to assess what other changes were made in this house, but a less blatant central gable would have been more appropriate to the size of the front door. The main street of Clinton presents a fascinating example of the "frosting" applied in Victorian times to much-earlier structures.

House

Essex, Connecticut
Built 1700s

Nothing is known about this
house except that it was originally a central hall Colonial
structure, built sometime in the
1700s. The carpenter who
added the trim was not only a
technical master of his craft, he
also had an exceedingly sure
eye for scale.

House

Tolland, Connecticut
Built 1850

Despite its Yankee setting in Tolland, Connecticut, there is little doubt that this house is a carpenter's free-wheeling interpretation of domestic architecture in the Swiss Alps. The top-heavy chalet exterior betrays little evidence of the graceful, interior floor plan. The house was built in 1850 by the grandfather of the present owner and is lovingly maintained. Except for modern conveniences, nothing has been changed inside or out. The original circular stained glass window still sheds its ruby glow over the second floor stair landing.

House

Thompson, Connecticut
Built c. 1840-1845

Here, indeed, are smiling lawns and a tasteful cottage photographed on a beautiful spring day in Thompson, Connecticut. Undoubtedly patterned after Design II in *Cottage Residences* (see pages 15, 84), this house bears a strong resemblance to the house in Portland, Maine, designed by Henry Rowe for John J. Brown (see page 41) and the Henry Mason Brooks House in Salem, Massachusetts (see pages 84-85). Elements excerpted from this plan can be found in many other houses in this book. It must have been one of Downing's most successful designs ever, and is thought to have been based on a plan by Davis.

Epilogue

Not long after Andrew Jackson Downing died in 1852 aboard a burning Hudson River ferryboat, this carved, marble urn was erected to his memory in the Washington Mall near the Smithsonian Institution. Only thirty-six years old at the time, his dramatic death made him even more of a celebrity.

Over the years the urn deteriorated and eventually went into storage to be repaired. There it stayed for fifty years. Finally, about 1970, it was returned to its original place overlooking the area where Downing had planned a beautiful woodland garden and park to serve as a foil for the Smithsonian and other government buildings.

Courtesy Smithsonian Institution, Washington, D.C.

Appendix of Tools

Foot treadle-operated scroll saw.

Foot treadle-operated mortising machine.

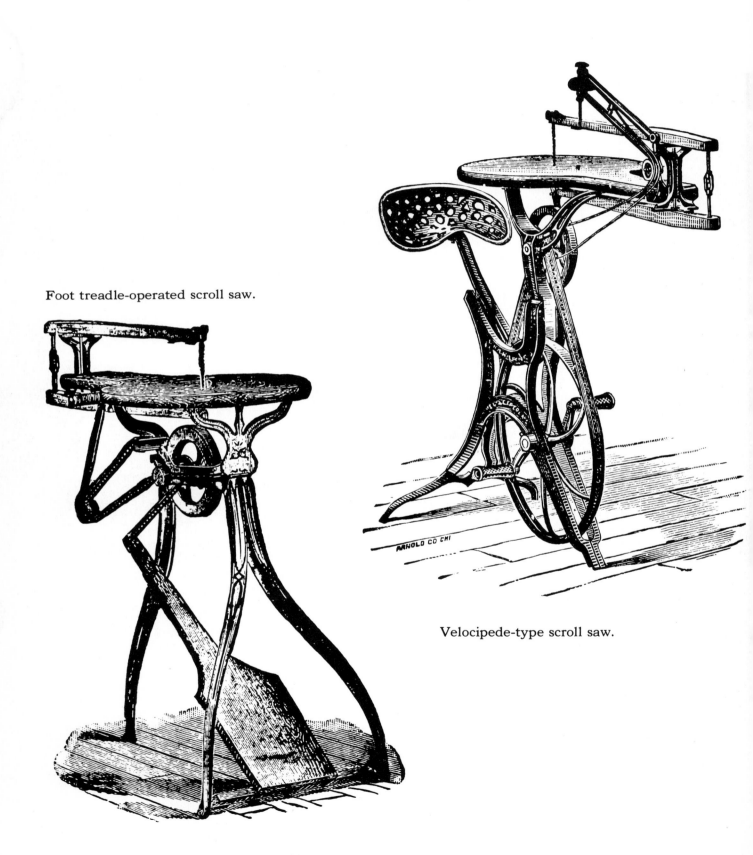

Foot treadle-operated scroll saw.

Velocipede-type scroll saw.

Hand-operated table circular saw.

Band saw.

Draw knife, used by carpenters and shingle makers.

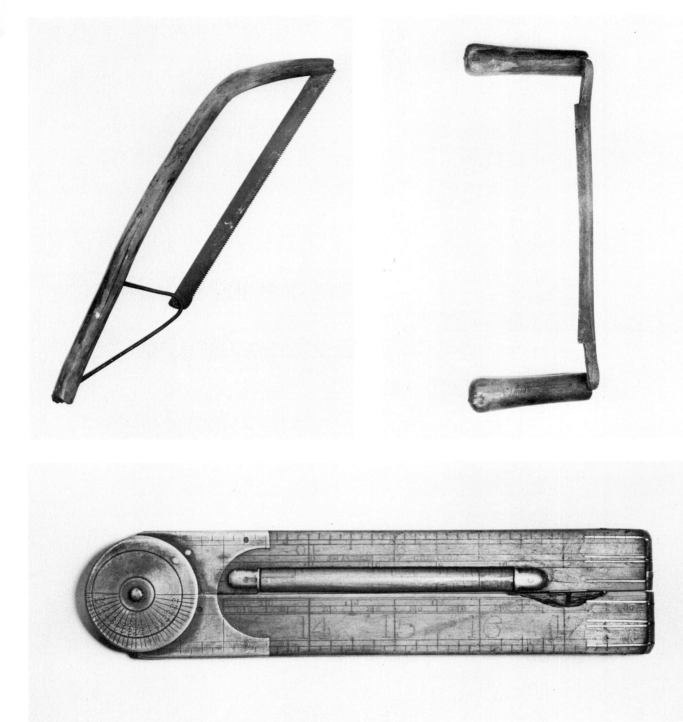

Molding rule, most commonly used.

Mortising marking gauge.

Washer cutter.

Thumb screw, a marking device.

Pump drill, very old device for boring holes.

Hand spiral auger, new model popular after 1800.

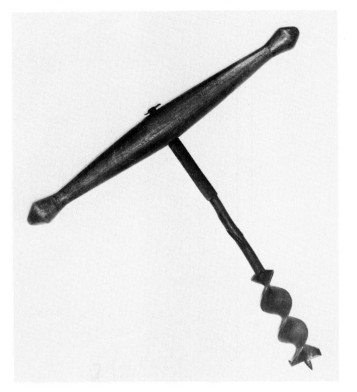

Bit brace and drill, eighteenth-century tool.

Molding plane.

Molding plane, or "hollow" or "plow" plane.

Jackplane, used to smooth very coarse boards.

Square groove router, used to smooth wood and also cut grooves.

Pad auger, used chiefly for tapping bevels.

Padlock.

Claw hammer, precursor of the adze, which was invented in 1840.

Ream awl, a boring tool used from the colonial period up to the late nineteenth century.

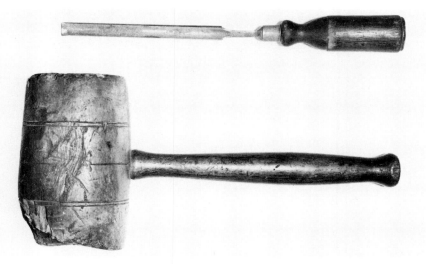

Wader mallet and wood gauge chisel, small carpentry tools.

Sources for information on tools:

Bealer, Alex. *Tools That Built America*. New York: Barre Publishing Co., 1975.

Blackburn, Graham. *An Illustrated Encyclopedia of Woodworking Handtools, Instruments and Devices*. New York: Simon & Schuster, 1974.

Selected Bibliography

Andrews, Wayne. *American Gothic*. New York: Random House, 1975.

Benjamin, Asher. *The Country Builders Assistant*. New York: The Architectural Book Publishing Company, 1917.

————. *House Carpenter*. Boston: Perkins & Marvin, 1839.

Bicknell, Amos. *Bicknell's Village Builder and Supplement*. New York: A.J. Bicknell & Co., 1872.

Burchard, John, and Bush-Brown, Albert. *The Architecture of America: A Social and Cultural History*. Boston: The Atlantic Monthly Press, 1961.

Card, Marian. "A.J. Davis and the Printed Specification." *College Art Journal* 22, no. 4 (Summer 1953), p. 357.

Carp, Ben. *Wood Motifs in American Domestic Architecture: Phantasy in Wood*. South Brunswick, N.J.: A.S. Barnes, 1966.

Clark, Kenneth McKensie. *The Gothic Revival: An Essay in the History of Taste*. New York: Charles Scribner & Sons, 1929.

Cleveland, Henry, Backus, William, and Backus, Samuel D. *Village and Farm Cottages*. New York: D. Appleton and Co., 1856.

Davidson, Ruth. "Roseland: A Gothic Revival Mansion." *Antiques Magazine*, no. 81 (May 1962), pp. 510-514.

Davies, Jane B. " 'We Can't Get on Without You,' Letters to Alexander J. Davis, Architect." *Columbia Library Columns* 16 (November 1966), p. 1.

Davis, Alexander Jackson. *Rural Residences*. Greenfield, Mass.: John Denio, 1837.

Downing, Andrew Jackson. *The Architecture of Country Houses*. New York: Appleton Publishers, 1850.

————. *Cottage Residences*. New York: Wiley & Putnam, 1842.

Early, James. *Romanticism and American Architecture*. New York: A.S. Barnes, 1965.

Eastlake, Charles L. *A History of the Gothic Revival*. New York: Leichester University Press, 1970.

Ferriday, Peter (ed.). *Victorian Architecture*. London: Jonathan Cape Ltd., 1963.

Fish, Carl Russell. *The Rise of the Common Man*. New York: The MacMillan Co., 1929.

Flaherty, Carol. "The Domestic Architecture of Downing." *The Old House Journal* 2, no. 10 (October 1974), p. 1.

Gillon, Edmund V., Jr. *Early Illustrations and Views of American Architecture*. New York: Dover Publications, 1971.

————, and Lancaster, Clay. *Victorian Houses: A Treasury of Lesser-Known Examples*. New York: Dover Publications, 1973.

Hitchcock, Henry-Russell. *19th and 20th Century Architecture.* Baltimore, Md.: Penguin Books, 1958.

Huntington, David Carew. *Art and the Excited Spirit.* Ann Arbor, Mich.: The University of Michigan Museum of Art, 1972.

Lancaster, Osbert. *Here of All Places.* Boston: Houghton Mifflin Co., 1958.

Loudon, John Claudius. *Encyclopaedia of Cottage, Farm and Villa Architecture and Furniture.* Edited by Mrs. Loudon. London: Longmans, 1867.

Lynes, Russell. *The Tastemakers.* New York: Harper, 1954.

Maas, John. *The Gingerbread Age.* New York: Bramhall House, 1952.

Mumford, Lewis. *Sticks and Stones.* New York: Dover Publications, 1924.

Pugin, Augustus Welby Northmore. *True Principles of Christian or Pointed Architecture.* London: Weale Publishers, 1841.

Root, Waverly, and deRochemont, Richard. *Eating in America: A History.* New York: William Morrow & Co., 1976.

Scully, Vincent. *The Shingle Style and the Stick Style.* New Haven, Conn.: Yale University Press, 1971.

————, and Downing, Antoinette. *The Architectural Heritage of Newport, Rhode Island 1640-1915.* Cambridge, Mass.: Harvard University Press, 1952.

Shaw, Edward. *Civil Architecture.* Boston: Marsh, Kapen & Lyon Company, 1834.

Sloan, Samuel. *The Model Architect.* Philadelphia: E.G. Jones Publishers, 1852.

Stanton, Phoebe. *The Gothic Revival and American Church Architecture: An Episode in Taste.* Baltimore, Md.: The Johns Hopkins University Press, 1968.

Tucci, Douglas Shand. *Ralph Adams Cram: American Medievalist.* Boston: The Boston Public Library Press, 1975.

Upjohn, Richard. *Upjohn's Rural Architecture.* New York: Putnam, 1852.

Vaux, Calvert. *Villas and Cottages.* 2d ed. New York: Harper, 1864.

"The Village Homes of England." *Studio Magazine.* Spring, 1912.

Wheeler, Gervase. *Rural Homes.* New York: Scribner, 1851.

Whiffen, Marcus. *American Architecture Since 1780: A Guide to the Styles.* Cambridge, Mass.: M.I.T. Press, 1969.

Appendix of Owners

Alvah Littlefield Cottage, Northampton, Massachusetts, Joseph Bohnak

Athenwood, Montpelier, Vermont, Mr. & Mrs. John Weaver

Buttonwood Farm, Chester, Vermont, Frederick and Carol Koledo of Springfield, Vermont

Commodore Charles Green House, South Windsor, Connecticut, Mr. & Mrs. Frederick Mahr

The Cottage, Fairfield, Connecticut, Mrs. Annie Sturges Bullard

Cottage, Rockport, Massachusetts, John Manera

Cottage, Exeter, New Hampshire, John Merkel

Cottage, Madison, Connecticut, Robert Strom

D. Flanders House, South Royalton, Vermont, M.K. and Ronald Desmarais

David Sikes House, Suffield, Connecticut, W.T. Sikes

Deacon Merrill C. Dodge House, Greenville, New Hampshire, Cecile and Everett Newell

Downing House, Andover, Massachusetts, Mr. & Mrs. George Ferance

Gaylord-Bassett Villa, Northampton, Massachusetts, Northampton School for Girls

George A. Pillsbury House, Concord, New Hampshire, Catherine L. Pappas

Henry Boody House, Brunswick, Maine, Bowdoin College

Henry Mason Brooks House, Salem, Massachusetts, Yousif Petrafhkewitch

Henry Thompson House, Thompsonville, Connecticut, Mr. & Mrs. Wilfrid Keller of Enfield, Connecticut

Homer Swift House, Milford, Connecticut, Mrs. Stanley Swift

Hopkins House, Northampton, Massachusetts, Smith College

House, Andover, Massachusetts, Augustine and Mary Sullivan

House, Andover, Massachusetts, M.D. Rosen of Ballardsville, Andover, Massachusetts

House, Castleton, Vermont, John Brooks

House, Chester, Vermont, Kent and Gale Ancliffe of Corinth, Vermont

House, Clinton, Connecticut, Charlotte Burnham

House, East Haddam, Connecticut, Casey Miller

House, Essex, Connecticut, Gifford Warner

House, Granville, Massachusetts, Mrs. Ernestine Reed of Westfield, Massachusetts

House, Northampton, Massachusetts, Clarke School for the Deaf

House, Peterborough, New Hampshire, Jack O'Loughlin of Nashua, New Hampshire

House, Tolland, Connecticut, Mrs. Aaron Pratt

James A. Latham House, Noank, Connecticut, Edward Ellis

James Hope House, Castleton, Vermont, Mrs. Theodore B. Holden

James Monroe House, Guilford, Connecticut, Mr. & Mrs. Richard McCurdy

John Adams House, Worthington, Massachusetts, Mrs. Carl Joslyn

John J. Brown House, Portland, Maine, A. Bodine Roll

Justin Smith Morrill Homestead, Strafford, Vermont, State of Vermont

The Kibbe House, Somers, Connecticut, John Myracle

Kingscote, Newport, Rhode Island, The Preservation Society of Newport County

Peter Davis House, Noank, Connecticut, John Wilber

Queset, North Easton, Massachusetts, William Ames

Reverend Edward Hall House, Providence, Rhode Island, Douglas and Charlotte Taber

Roseland, Woodstock, Connecticut, Society for the Preservation of New England Antiquities

Stephen Colton House, Longmeadow, Massachusetts, Estate of Mabel Buxton

The Stone Cottage, Middletown, Connecticut, Wesleyan University

Townsend House, Windsor, Vermont, Mrs. George Orebaugh

The Wedding Cake House, Kennebunkport, Maine, Mrs. Harold Lord

Wetmore-Weeks House, Middletown, Connecticut, Wesleyan University

William A. Goodwin House, Portland, Maine, Dr. & Mrs. Jeremy Morton

William Cullen Bryant Homestead, Cummington, Massachusetts, State of Massachusetts

William J. Rotch, Esq. House, New Bedford, Massachusetts, John Bullard

Acknowledgments

Acknowledgment and warmest thanks go to the following people for their help with this book:

Ernestine Potter, Guilford, Connecticut

Betsy and Hubbard Cobb, Old Lyme, Connecticut

Nancy Page, Hyannis, Massachusetts

Ruth Lodge, Chappaqua, New York

Jake Ehlers, Chappaqua, New York

June McC. and William S. White, Madison, Connecticut

Irene and Edwin Lanham, Clinton, Connecticut

Jean and Seward Hull, Jr., Clinton, Connecticut

Edna Hyer Pardo, Clinton, Connecticut

Mary Jane Higby and Guy Sorel, Clinton, Connecticut

Katherine Mort Lupone, Guilford Keeping Society, Guilford, Connecticut

Mrs. Leonard J. Panaggio, The Preservation Society of Newport County, Newport, Rhode Island

John A. Cherol, Registrar, The Preservation Society of Newport County, Newport, Rhode Island

Sarah Lutzman, Assistant Registrar, The Preservation Society of Newport County, Newport, Rhode Island

Earle G. Shettleworth, Jr., Director, Maine Historic Preservation Commission, Augusta, Maine

Robert L. Bradley, PhD, Architectural Historian, Maine Historic Preservation Commission, Augusta, Maine

Phyllis Norton Mahoney, Cambridge, Massachusetts

Dean and Mrs. Paul Nyhus, Bowdoin College, Brunswick, Maine

A.B. Van Liew, President, Heritage Foundation of Rhode Island, Providence, Rhode Island

Mrs. Deborah D. Neu, Providence Preservation Society, Providence, Rhode Island

William O'Malley, Avery Library, Columbia University, New York, New York

George Campbell, Stonington, Connecticut

Mrs. Richard C. Donnelly, Chairperson, Historic Sites, Madison Historical Society, Madison, Connecticut

Wilma Barrett, Town Clerk, Chester, Vermont

Mr. and Mrs. Paul Adams, Chester, Vermont

Joellyn Kuhnlein and Barbara Ann Cleary, Greater Middletown Preservation Trust, Middletown, Connecticut

William Grover, AIA, Essex, Connecticut

Dorothy Cramer, Historical Society, Noank, Connecticut

Gary Frohlich, Guilford, Connecticut

Barbara Adams, Department of History of Art, Yale University, New Haven, Connecticut

Jonathan Heller, Archives Technician, National Archives, Washington, D.C.

James Steed, Smithsonian Archives, Washington, D.C.

Capt. John Wilber, Noank, Connecticut

Mrs. Wheeler Hunt, Fairfield Historical Society, Fairfield, Connecticut

Gerald Ward, Garvan Collection, Yale University, New Haven, Connecticut

Mary Flynn, Andover, Massachusetts

John C. Perry, Chairman, New Hampshire State Historical Commission, Concord, New Hampshire

James L. Garvin, Curator, New Hampshire Historical Society, Concord, New Hampshire

Marilyn Blackwell, Vermont Historical Society, Montpelier, Vermont

Richard C. Kugler, Old Dartmouth, Historical Society Whaling Museum, New Bedford, Massachusetts

Mrs. Arthur R. Norton, Reference Librarian, Essex Institute, Salem, Massachusetts

Martha Larsen, Curator, North Andover Historical Society, North Andover, Massachusetts

Mrs. Ruth E. Wilber, The Northampton Historical Society, Northampton, Massachusetts

Nancy Stack, Senior Planner, Northampton Historical Commission, Northampton, Massachusetts

Eric Gilbertson, Assistant Director, Division for Historic Preservation, Montpelier, Vermont

Jane McLuckie Lendway, Architectural Historian, Division for Historic Preservation, Montpelier, Vermont

Cherrie Child, Carmel Valley, California

Miss Marie E. Griswold, Guilford, Connecticut

Carl Mangs, Branford, Connecticut

Georgianna Brush, Executive Director, Historic District, Windsor, Vermont

Agnes Barry, Madison, Connecticut

Frederick P. Murphy, Jr., Madison, Connecticut

John P. Brucksch, Curator, Andover Historical Society, Andover, Massachusetts

Beale Hughes, Orinda, California

Constance Gentry, San Jose, California

Elliott Hess, New York, New York

Special mention must be made of the exceptional generosity and help of the following:

Professor William H. Pierson, Jr., Williamstown, Massachusetts, and Bryant F. Tolles, Jr., Director, Essex Institute, Salem, Massachusetts, both of whom gave us access to unpublished material.

Paul Kebabian, Bailey Library, University of Vermont, Burlington, Vermont, who assisted us in tracking down old tools, as did William Worthington, Museum Technician, Division of Mechanical and Civil Engineering, Smithsonian Institution, Washington, D.C.

David Chase, Deputy Director, Historical Preservation Commission, Providence, Rhode Island, who worked overtime to assist with information on the E.B. Hall House.

Juliet H. Mofford, North Andover, Massachusetts, whose detailed research was extremely valuable.

Professor Samuel M. Green, Wesleyan University, Middletown, Connecticut, for early interest and much appreciated help with the project.

Jacqueline Miller-Rice for her talented assistance with special photographic details.

Michael McMahon for his fine photography of the engravings.

My editors at the Whitney Library of Design: Sarah Bodine, Susan Davis, and Ann Titus.

Grateful thanks go to those who housed and cosseted us and did a million other things to keep the project going. They include:

Edna Shilling, Branford, Connecticut
Mrs. Fred B. Korsmeyer, Madison, Connecticut
Frances King Blaha, Madison, Connecticut
Mary and Theodor Pfeil, Port Clyde, Maine
Kim Chaffee, Amherst, Massachusetts

I am very grateful to Stephanie Cottrell, Madison, Connecticut, for checking town hall records and to Kathleen D'Amico, Clinton, Connecticut, for her secretarial aid with the manuscript.

Also Paul Molumphy, M.D., Richard Selzer, M.D., and Elizabeth B. Hull for reasons they know best.

Finally for our families who listened, encouraged, advised, offered solace, and held their tempers:

Walcott Hamilton
Gertrude Sherman Hamilton
Eleanor Bartlett Skinner
Cush McArdle
My son John
My husband Jack

Index

Edited by Sarah Bodine, Susan Davis, and Ann Titus
Designed by James Craig
Composed in 12 point Bookman